EARTH FILES

DESERTS

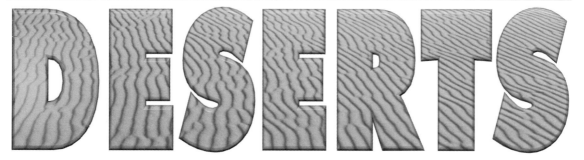

EARTH FILES – DESERTS
was produced by

David West ⚇ Children's Books

7 Princeton Court
55 Felsham Road
London SW15 1AZ

Editor: James Pickering
Picture Research: Carrie Haines

First published in Great Britain in 2002 by
Heinemann Library, Halley Court, Jordan Hill,
Oxford OX2 8EJ, a division of Reed Educational and
Professional Publishing Limited.

OXFORD MELBOURNE AUCKLAND
JOHANNESBURG BLANTYRE GABORONE
IBADAN PORTSMOUTH (NH) USA CHICAGO

06 05 04 03 02
10 9 8 7 6 5 4 3 2 1

ISBN 0 431 15624 7 (HB)
ISBN 0 431 15631 X (PB)

British Library Cataloguing in Publication Data

Ganeri, Anita
Deserts. - (Earth Files)
1. Deserts - Juvenile literature
2. Desert ecology - Juvenile literature
I. Title
551.4'15

PHOTO CREDITS :
Abbreviations: t-top, m-middle, b-bottom, r-right,
l-left, c-centre.

Front cover, 3, 4t & 21tl, 4-5b & 14-15b, 4tr &
18bl, 4br, 7br, 8bl, 9br, 12bl, 14m, 14-15t, 15 all,
18br, 20-21b, 21tr, bl & br, 24-25b, 26 all, 29tr -
Corbis Images. 6-7b (Lee Frost 2001), 10-11t (P.
Verbeeck), 10-11b, 17b (Geoff Renner), 11ml, 12-13t,
13br, 20bl (Tony Waltham), 18-19t (Fred Friberg),
23br (Sylvain Grandadam), 24tl (Ian Griffiths), 24-
25t (D. Janet), 27br (Robert Francis), 28b (Peter
Ryan), 28-29t (Doug Traverso), 16-17, 20tr, 22mr,
22-23b, 23bl - Robert Harding Picture Library. 11br,
19tr, 22-23t, 29b (François Gohier), 17tr (Adrian
Warren), 18bm (M. Watson), 19ml (Ken Lucas), 19bl
(John Daniels), 19br (Kenneth W. Fink), 25b (Y.
Arthus - Bertrand), 28ml (Richard Waller) - Ardea
London Ltd.

Printed and bound in Italy

*An explanation of difficult words can be
found in the glossary on page 31.*

EARTH FILES

DESERTS

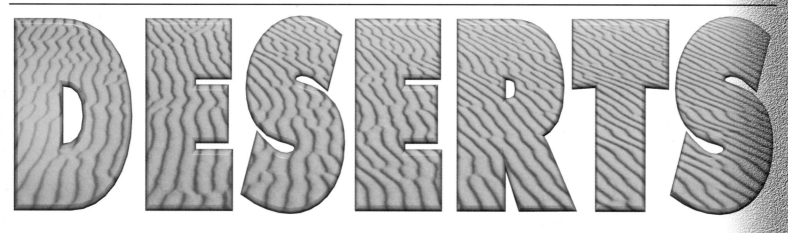

Anita Ganeri

Heinemann
LIBRARY

CONTENTS

During a rare summer shower of rain, some deserts burst into bloom. Seeds that have lain buried for months, or even years, suddenly sprout and flower.

INTRODUCTION

Few places on Earth are as mysterious as the great deserts. They are the driest places on the planet, usually pictured as bleak expanses of scorching sand and dramatic scenery, with such a harsh climate that nothing can survive for long. But are deserts really as inhospitable as they first seem? Despite the hostile conditions, the deserts are home for a surprising number of plants, animals and people. They have the know-how to stay alive, often against the odds.

Reptiles, such as this blue-tongued skink, are well suited to desert life. They use the desert sun to warm their bodies so that they can be active.

Over millions of years, wind and water have created dramatic desert landscapes, from great seas of sand to mighty mountains. Deserts have a stark beauty, but they are dangerous places to be.

Deserts cover about a third of the Earth's land surface. There are deserts in Asia, Africa, North and South America, and even in freezing Antarctica. In fact, Europe is the only continent without any desert.

DRY AS A BONE

Deserts are places which receive less than 250 millimetres of rain per year. Scientists also measure the balance of water in a desert, using an aridity (dryness) index. They compare the yearly rainfall with the amount of water that evaporates in a year. The immense Sahara Desert in Africa scores an amazing 200 on the aridity index. This means that it loses 200 times more water than it receives.

NORTH AMERICA

1

2

3

Tropic of Cancer

Equator

SOUTH AMERICA

Tropic of Capricorn

4

5

6

Over three-quarters of the scorching Sahara Desert receives less than 100 millimetres of rain per year.

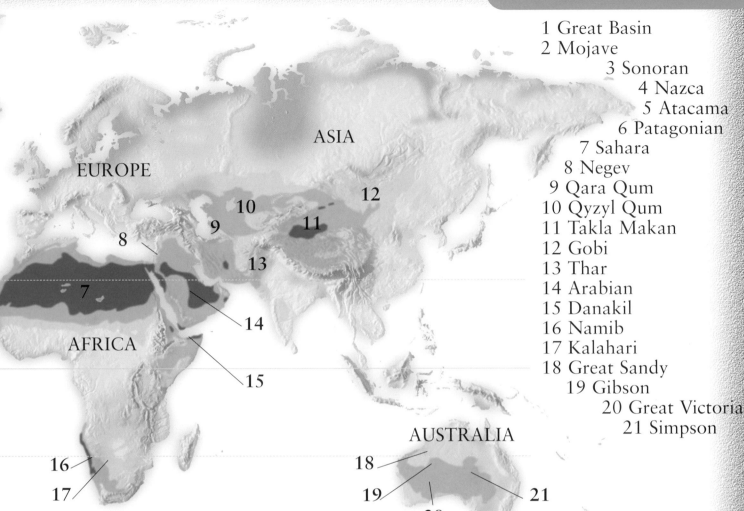

ASIA

EUROPE

AFRICA

AUSTRALIA

1 Great Basin
2 Mojave
3 Sonoran
4 Nazca
5 Atacama
6 Patagonian
7 Sahara
8 Negev
9 Qara Qum
10 Qyzyl Qum
11 Takla Makan
12 Gobi
13 Thar
14 Arabian
15 Danakil
16 Namib
17 Kalahari
18 Great Sandy
19 Gibson
20 Great Victoria
21 Simpson

■ The driest deserts, where it hardly ever rains.

■ Deserts that have enough rain for some plants to grow.

Semi-deserts, with enough rain for shrubby plants to grow.

Frozen wastes

Strictly speaking, Antarctica counts as a desert because it is so dry. On average, this freezing cold continent receives less than 50 millimetres of rain or snow a year. There are some places where no rain has fallen for two million years.

Most of the water in Antarctica is locked up in ice.

There are different types of desert, depending on where they form. Some deserts lie far inland; others form along the coast. Their location affects the formation of rainclouds and rainfall, which is the reason why they are so dry.

DESERT LANDSCAPES

Different deserts vary a great deal in appearance. Only about a quarter of the world's deserts are sandy. Most deserts are made up of vast stretches of stony or pebbly ground. Others are salty, or covered in ancient volcanic rock.

The Sonoran Desert stretches down from the south-western USA into Baja California along the coast of Mexico.

TROPICAL DESERTS

Tropical deserts occur on either side of the Equator where warm air from the tropics cools and sinks. This creates an area of high pressure which brings hot, dry weather.

Sandy desert
The Arabic name for a sandy desert is *erg*. This is a huge sea of sand which the wind blows into rolling dunes.

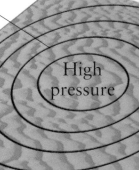

High pressure

Cold current

COASTAL DESERTS

Cold ocean currents flowing along the coast cool the air blowing inland. Cool air can hold very little moisture and so the wind is too dry to form rainclouds.

Rocky volcanic
In some deserts, the landscape features volcanic rocks and the stumps of ancient, extinct volcanoes. Two massive volcanic blocks form mountains in the Sahara Desert.

Salt flats
Some deserts are covered in vast, flat salty plains. They are created when water evaporates in the sun, leaving the salt behind.

INLAND DESERTS
Some deserts form inland, far from the coast. Winds blowing in from the sea usually carry moisture with them. But any rain has fallen long before they reach this far inland.

Rocky desert
In Arabic, *hammada* means an area of rocky desert, stripped bare of sand and dust by the wind.

Stony desert
Reg is the Arabic word for a flat desert plain, covered in tightly-packed stones and pebbles.

Dry air

RAIN-SHADOW DESERTS
As air rises over the mountains, it cools and forms rainclouds. By the time the clouds reach the other side, they have lost all their rain, creating a rain-shadow desert.

Rain falls on windward side of mountains.

Space travel

A playa is a flat plain formed when a salt lake dries up in the desert. (*Playa* is the Spanish word for 'shore'.) One large playa, called Rogers Lake, in the Mojave Desert, California, USA, has been used for space shuttle landings. The shuttle glides in to land, and travels for several kilometres along the ground before it reaches a standstill.

The space shuttle landing.

All deserts are dry and dusty because of low rainfall. The lack of rainclouds mean deserts may be scorching hot by day because there is no shade. At night, the temperature falls rapidly as heat is lost from the ground.

HOT AND COLD

The hottest, driest deserts lie on either side of the Equator in the tropics. Daytime temperatures in the Sahara can reach a sizzling 50°C. But some deserts, such as the Gobi Desert, have very cold winters, with temperatures plummetting to a freezing -20°C.

Sweeping in from the desert, a duststorm can be terrifying. The thick cloud of dust creates havoc, bringing transport to a standstill and causing breathing difficulties. Each year, up to 200 million tonnes of dust is produced by the Sahara Desert alone.

DESERT DISTORTIONS

The desert can play tricks on your eyes. You may be fooled into thinking you can see water on the horizon. In fact, this is a mirage. It happens when a layer of cold air traps a layer of hot air next to the ground. The layers bend light coming from the cold air, making it appear like water.

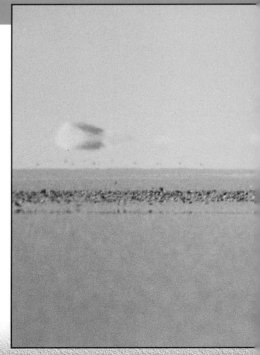

Light bends as it passes through the layers of air

Cold air

Mirage

Hot air

Some deserts are bitterly cold in winter, with heavy snowfall and frequent blizzards, and temperatures falling well below freezing. High-lying areas of land may have snowstorms at any time of the year.

STORMY WEATHER

Strong winds are common in the desert because there are few plants to slow them down. The wind races over the ground, whipping up choking clouds of sand and dust. Sometimes the sand or dust is so thick that it is impossible to see.

Driest desert

Although the Atacama Desert lies along the South American coast, it is the driest desert in the world. In some places, no rain at all has ever been recorded. Other places may experience a freak downpour of rain once every ten years.

The bone-dry Atacama Desert in Chile.

A mirage in the Sahara Desert.

11

The most famous desert features are rolling sand seas and towering dunes. Sand is made up of tiny rock fragments, eroded, or worn away, by the weather. These are picked up by the wind and dumped in the desert.

WIND AND SAND

The wind plays a major part in shaping the desert landscape. As it blows across the ground, it piles the sand up into great wave-like dunes. The largest sand dunes stand 200 metres tall and measure 900 metres across. Each dune contains millions of tonnes of sand.

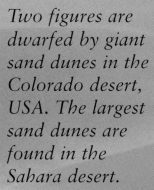

Two figures are dwarfed by giant sand dunes in the Colorado desert, USA. The largest sand dunes are found in the Sahara desert.

The wind blows the sand into a variety of patterns. A wind blowing in one direction creates a series of ridges and furrows.

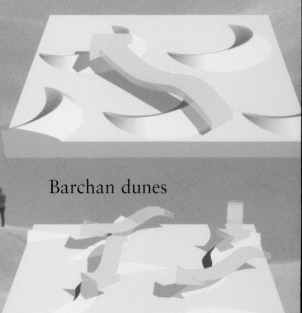

Barchan dunes

Seif dunes

Seif dunes (seif is the Arabic word for sword) form when the wind blows from different directions.

SEAS AND SAND

Most sand dunes are gathered together in vast ergs, or seas of sand. As the wind drifts and shifts direction, it sculpts the sand into different shapes. Huge sand seas cover about a quarter of the world's deserts and are mostly found in Arabia, North Africa and Central Asia. The largest of all is the Rub al Khali, or Empty Quarter, in the Arabian Desert. It covers an area of 560,000 square kilometres, about the size of France. In between the dunes are sandy plains, or stretches of stony desert.

SHAPES IN THE SAND

The shape of a sand dune depends on the speed and direction of the wind. A barchan dune forms when the wind blows steadily in one direction. If there is an obstacle, such as a boulder or bush, the flow slows down and the sand builds up into a crescent-shaped dune. More complex star-shaped dunes are formed by shifting winds.

Star dune

Creeping dunes

Some sand dunes, such as star dunes, are quite stable. But others, such as barchan dunes, can shift by as much as 50 metres a year. As the wind blows sand over the top of the dune, the dune creeps forward, burying villages, oases and roads in its path.

A sand dune blocking a road.

Over millions of years, the desert landscape is dramatically shaped by the effects of the wind, the extreme changes in temperature, and the rare but torrential downpours of rain. This weathering process is called erosion.

CARVING SHAPES

By day, desert rocks expand in the heat. At night, they contract in the cold. This puts the rocks under extreme stress and causes them to crack. Water is also important in shaping the landscape. During a rare downpour, flash floods create temporary rivers. These sweep along stones and boulders which scrape and scour the rocks.

The combined forces of wind and rain carve out dramatic natural arches in the desert.

Mesas are towering, flat-topped sandstone mountains, left behind when the land around them has been eroded by the wind and rain. In Spanish, mesa means table.

MUSHROOM ROCKS

In a sandstorm, the wind sends sand grains bouncing along about a metre or two above the ground. This is called saltation. This means that as the wind blasts the sand against a rock, the sand scours away at the base but cannot reach the top. Over the years, this creates a striking mushroom-shaped rock.

Spectacular limestone pillars in Bryce Canyon, Utah, USA are formed by the effects of wind, snow and rain over thousands of years.

Mushroom rocks in Goblin Valley, Utah.

Bridges may be carved out by the action of rivers which have long since dried up.

Painted Desert

Over thousands of years, erosion by the wind and rain has exposed beautiful, multi-coloured layers of rock in the Painted Desert, Arizona, USA. The layers are made of ancient clay, sand and shale which were first laid down about 70 million years ago.

A canyon's wall reveals colourful layers of rock.

15

Water is essential for survival in the desert. Although deserts look barren and dry, there is water to be found. Some falls as rain and fills dry river beds. Some seeps up from deep underground.

OASIS IN THE DESERT

Where underground water comes to the surface, it creates a rare, fertile patch of land called an oasis. Here people can bring their animals to drink, and cultivate crops, such as palm trees. Water can be pumped from the oasis to water farmers' fields.

WATER FROM UNDERGROUND

Rain soaks through tiny pores, or holes, in the rock. Rocks that hold water are called aquifers. The water flows underground until it reaches a fault, or split, in the layers of rock. If the pressure is strong enough, the water is forced to the surface to create an oasis. Wells are often drilled through the rocks to reach the aquifer.

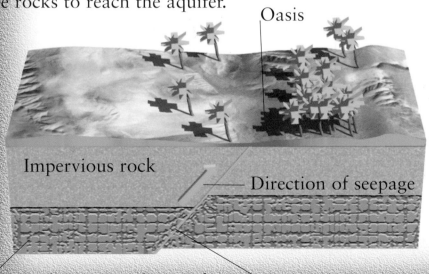

Oasis

Impervious rock

Direction of seepage

Water-bearing rock (aquifer)　Fault

Palm trees are an ideal crop for cultivating at an oasis. They provide dates to eat, leaves for thatching roofs and making baskets, and fibres for making rope.

Water eggs

The San people of the Kalahari Desert have an ingenious way of carrying water on hunting trips. They suck up underground water through hollow reeds, and store it in empty ostrich eggshells.

Ostrich eggshell water-carriers.

WADIS AND FLASH FLOODS

Wadis, or desert river beds, are usually dry. But, during a heavy storm, a large amount of water falls very quickly, filling the wadi to overflowing. The river bursts its banks, causing a flash flood. Flash floods can occur almost without any warning, sweeping away everything in their path, including large boulders and even people.

Within minutes, a wadi can turn from a dry river bed into a raging torrent. The rain may have fallen some distance away, and the first warning of a raging flash flood may be the roar of the water approaching at great speed.

Despite the hostile conditions in deserts, many animals have adapted to life there. Many animals survive the heat by only coming out at night. They spend the day resting in the shade of rocks or plants, or in cool burrows under the baking desert ground.

STAYING ALIVE

Desert animals use a wide range of survival skills to cope with the problems of staying cool and finding enough to drink and eat. Many have developed special features to help them stay alive.

The Peringuey's viper uses a sidewinding movement to cross the sand. Its body touches the sand for just a few seconds, so it does not overheat.

Desert predators get water from the bodies of the prey they eat. To warn off predators, the frilled lizard spreads out its neck frill to make it look bigger and fiercer.

Many desert reptiles are active in the day, basking in the morning sun to warm their bodies up. The blue-tongued skink sticks out its tongue to scare away predators, such as birds and mammals.

Camels' long legs hold their bodies off the hot ground as they walk, and their wide, flat feet are good for travelling over soft sand.

At the first sign of rain, spadefoot toads find a pool and lay their eggs. They spend the rest of the time asleep in cool, underground burrows.

Gerbils come out at night to feed on seeds. If a predator comes close, they leap away on their long back legs.

Desert dinosaurs!
Thousands of fossils of dinosaurs and other prehistoric animals have been found in the Gobi Desert. They have been perfectly preserved by the dry heat and soft sand.

Fossilized dinosaur eggs.

SHIPS OF THE DESERT
Camels are perfectly suited to desert life because they can go for days without water. They can also survive for weeks without food, by using the fat stored in their humps.

Large ears help the fennec fox to lose excess heat and listen out for its prey.

19

Desert plants also have to survive on a limited water supply. Some have long or spreading roots to soak up water from a large area. Others have specially adapted stems and leaves for saving and storing water.

DEW DRINKING

The weird-looking welwitschia plant grows in the Namib Desert. It has long, strap-like leaves which become split and frayed in the wind. The leaves collect tiny droplets of dew and channel them into the ground to be stored in the plant's huge root.

Baobab trees have expanding trunks that swell with water when it rains. During the dry season, the tree lives off this built-in water supply.

Welwitschia plants are actually dwarf trees. The ragged leaves lie curled around the stunted trunk.

Some giant cacti can grow up to 18 metres long and weigh about ten tonnes. Most of this weight is water.

Cacti are the most famous of all desert plants. But they only grow in the deserts of North America.

PRICKLES AND SPINES

Cacti can store water in their stems, and have a waxy skin to stop moisture escaping. Their leaves are fine spines which lose very little water into the air.

Some desert plants lie buried as seeds to avoid the dry weather. They can stay like this for months, or years. As soon as it rains, they start to sprout and the desert bursts into bloom.

Tumbleweed is blown across the desert.

Tumbleweed

Tumbleweed is a plant that breaks from its roots and dries into a tangle of branches. It rolls long distances in the wind, scattering its seeds as it goes.

21

Some 650 million people live in or near deserts. They have learned how to live with the hostile desert weather, and to find enough to eat and drink.

ON THE MOVE

Many desert people are nomads, people who wander from place to place in search of food and water. To suit their lifestyle, they need shelters that are easy to move. Many live in tents, made from animal hide, wool and hair. The tents are designed for maximum protection against the desert wind and extremes of heat and cold.

Many people of the Sahara and Arabian deserts are Muslims who follow the religion of Islam. They build mosques in the desert, where they can worship.

Many nomads live in tents, which are light, easy to carry from place to place and can be pitched quickly.

Winters in the Gobi Desert can be bitterly cold. Mongol nomads live in circular tents, called gers, made from felt stretched over a wooden frame to keep in the warmth.

The city of Phoenix in Arizona, USA, relies for water on the Colorado River. So much water has been pumped from the river that it is running dry.

TOWNS AND TRADE

There are some permanent towns and settlements in the desert. Most have grown up around oases, where there is a regular water supply. Some larger towns have markets where nomadic people come to trade.

The Tuareg

About a million Tuareg people live in the Sahara Desert. For centuries, they lived as nomads, raising camels, sheep, goats and cattle, and guiding traders. Today, their traditional lifestyle is under threat as vehicles have replaced camels, and drought has reduced their grazing land.

A Tuareg nomad.

23

Stretching over a third of Africa, the Sahara is the largest desert in the world. It covers nine million square kilometres, and is as big as the USA. *Sahara* is the Arabic word for desert.

About six thousand years ago, the Sahara was lush and green. Rock paintings found at Tassili, Algeria, show that, at that time, herds of elephants and giraffes roamed the land.

The Sahara stretches from the Atlantic Ocean in the west to the Red Sea in the east, and from the Mediterranean in the north down through Africa.

SAHARAN LANDSCAPE

About one fifth of the Sahara is erg, or sand seas. In the centre are mountains, formed by ancient volcanic eruptions. Most of the Sahara is reg, or flat, stony plains.

A camel caravan, loaded with goods for trade, crosses the Sahara. Although they are used less often today, camels are able to cross desert that no vehicles can navigate.

CAMEL CARAVANS

For centuries, important trade routes criss-crossed the Sahara. Camel caravans, hundreds of animals strong, carried goods, such as dates, salt and gold. The Tuareg people (see page 23) traded in salt, one of the desert's most precious resources. The salt was mined in Niger, and shaped into hard cones. Then Tuareg caravans carried it across hundreds of kilometres of scorching desert, to trade for sugar, tea and grain.

Paris–Dakar rally

The Paris–Dakar Rally is one of the most gruelling sporting events. Each year, more than a hundred drivers set off on the three-week, 1,300-kilometre long race.

Cars, trucks and motorbikes travel straight across the Sahara, testing the vehicles to their limit. They have to rely on satellite systems to navigate the vast stretches of sand.

Competitors can find it soft going in the Paris–Dakar Rally.

Some extremely valuable resources lie buried beneath the desert sand. They include salt, oil and many different types of precious metals and minerals. Modern technology has made it possible to extract these rich resources.

DRILLING FOR OIL

Huge quantities of oil have been found trapped in the deserts of the Middle East. Oil was first struck in the Arabian Desert in the 1930s. Today, this desert produces more than a quarter of the world's oil, making countries like Saudi Arabia extremely rich.

Salt has been mined in the desert for thousands of years. Lake beds fill with water when it rains, and the salt settles on the bottom. When the water evaporates, a thick layer of salt is left behind.

In the Arabian Desert the oil has to be pumped out of the ground and piped across the desert to an oil refinery.

MINING FOR METALS

Large stores of precious metals are found in many deserts. The Sahara is rich in iron. Gold and silver are mined in Australia. To extract these metals, huge areas of the desert are turned into mines. But extracting and processing the metal ores has a long-term, devastating effect, destroying the landscape and causing serious problems of pollution.

The vast Chuquicamata copper mine in the Atacama Desert in South America produces most of the world's copper. It is the world's largest copper mine.

Diamonds in the desert

One of the world's richest areas for diamonds is the Diamond Coast, where the Namib Desert meets the sea. Machines plough through thousands of tonnes of sand every day, to reach the diamond-rich gravel. This is sent to a processing plant where the diamonds are then extracted.

Before they are cut and polished, diamonds have a surprisingly dull appearance.

Around the world, deserts appear to be growing as land at the edges is overfarmed or overgrazed, and reduced to dust. Efforts are being made to stop the spread and turn the desert green.

A healthy-looking field of sugarcane in Egypt. Water is pumped from the River Nile to irrigate farmers' fields.

SPREADING DESERTS

Desertification (the process by which deserts spread) can happen naturally because of climate changes. People are adding to the problem by overusing the land at the desert margins.

The desert is gradually closing in on this small farm in Saudi Arabia. Holding the sand back is very difficult.

Tree roots help to bind the dry soil together. If the trees are cut down for firewood, the soil is easily blown away. In some deserts, new trees are being planted to replace them.

GREENING THE DESERT

In some deserts, farmers irrigate the land with huge, rotating sprinkler systems. These create circular, green fields, like the ones shown below, where crops such as wheat can be grown.

This method of irrigation uses water pumped from underground aquifers. The danger is that the water is being used up faster than it can be replaced.

Solar power

In the future, the desert sun could become the desert's most important renewable resource. Some solar power stations are already in use to harness the Sun's power. This is converted into electricity which can be used to heat and pump water cheaply.

An experimental solar power station in the Arizona desert.

THE BIGGEST DESERT	The Sahara is the world's biggest desert, covering an area of about nine million square kilometres. It covers a third of Africa, and is bounded to the north by the Atlas Mountains and the Mediterranean Sea, to the west by the Atlantic Ocean and to the east by the Red Sea.
THE COLDEST DESERT	Apart from Antarctica, the coldest desert is the Gobi. It is also the most northerly. In summer, the desert is scorching hot with temperatures reaching 45°C in July. But the Gobi suffers from freezing winters, with temperatures plummetting to - 40°C in January.
THE HOTTEST DESERT	The highest temperature ever recorded on Earth was 58°C in the shade, in the Sahara Desert at Al' Aziziyah, Libya. Summers are scorching hot in the Sahara, particularly in June, July and August. But at night, the heat is quickly lost and temperatures drop sharply to well below freezing.
THE DRIEST DESERT	Parts of the Atacama Desert along the coast of Chile get virtually no rain at all, just scattered freak showers that occur every ten years or so. Further inland, above a height of about 3,350 metres, rain and snow sometimes fall between January and March.
THE FOGGIEST DESERT	The Namib Desert lies along the coast of southern Africa. A cold ocean current cools the air above it, producing thick fog which rolls in off the sea. Animals, such as the darkling beetle, rely on the fog for water. Fog condenses on its body and trickles into its mouth.
THE RICHEST DESERT	More than a quarter of the world's oil reserves are found in the gigantic oil fields which lie under the Arabian Desert. The income from oil has made the region's countries, such as Saudi Arabia, among the richest in the world.
THE SANDIEST DESERT	The Takla Makan Desert in China is one of the world's largest sandy deserts. In places, the sand is 300 metres thick. The wind piles it into seas of crescent-shaped dunes. Very few plants grow in the Takla Makan because they cannot take root in the shifting sand.

GLOSSARY

adapted

Having skills or features which help an animal, plant or person to survive in a particular place.

condenses

When water vapour gas cools and turns into liquid water.

drought

A long period with little or no rain.

erosion

The process by which the landscape is carved into shape by the forces of the wind, water, heat and cold.

evaporates

When liquid water is heated and turns into a gas called water vapour.

high pressure

A place where cool air sinks and presses on the ground. High pressure usually brings sunny, dry weather.

impervious

A substance, such as some types of rock, which water cannot pass through.

irrigate

To bring water from a river, lake or well to water the land.

mirage

An optical illusion, usually similar to a pool of water, caused by light from the sky being bent by layers of hot and cold desert air.

oasis

A lush, fertile patch in the desert where water seeps up from underground. Crops can grow in oases, and desert animals and people can eat and drink there.

predators

Animals that hunt and feed on other animals.

prey

Animals that are hunted and eaten by other animals.